FIGHTER PLANES

BY RYAN NAGELHOUT

Gareth Stevens
PUBLISHING

HOT TOPICS

Please visit our website, www.garethstevens.com. For a free color catalog of all our high-quality books, call toll free 1-800-542-2595 or fax 1-877-542-2596.

Nagelhout, Ryan.
Fighter planes / by Ryan Nagelhout.
p. cm. — (Mighty military machines)
Includes index.
ISBN 978-1-4824-2118-7 (pbk.)
ISBN 978-1-4824-2117-0 (6-pack)
ISBN 978-1-4824-2119-4 (library binding)
1. Fighter planes — Juvenile literature. I. Nagelhout, Ryan. II. Title.
UG1242.F5 N34 2015
623.7—d23

First Edition

Published in 2015 by
Gareth Stevens Publishing
111 East 14th Street, Suite 349
New York, NY 10003

Designer: Nicholas Domiano
Editor: Ryan Nagelhout

Photo credits: Cover (background) Ensuper/Shutterstock.com; cover (series logo) Makhnach_S/Shutterstock.com; cover, p. 1 Chris Parypa Photography/Shutterstock.com; pp. 5, 22, 23, 24 Strocktrek Images/Getty Images; p. 6 Library of Congress/Photo Researchers/Getty Images; p. 7 Chris Maddaloni/CQ-Roll Call Group/Getty Images; p. 8 Dennis K. Johnson/Lonely Planet Images/Getty Images; p. 9 Roger Viollet/Getty Images; p. 10 Popperfoto/Getty Images; p. 11 Royal Air Force Museum/Hulton Archive/ Getty Images; p. 13 (P-47 Thunderbolt) PhotoQuest/Archive Photos/Getty Images; p. 13 (Messerschmitt) Kogo/Wikimedia Commons; p. 13 (Japanese Zero) Stahlkocher/Wikimedia Commons; p. 13 (P-51 Mustang) Diane Miller/Photolibrary/Getty Images; p. 15 ERIC FEFERBERG/AFP/Getty Images; p. 17 Interim Archives/Archive Photos/Getty Images; p. 19 Erik Simonsen/Photographer's Choice/Getty Images; p. 21 JACK GUEZ/AFP/Getty Images; pp. 27, 25, 29 Fort Worth Star-Telegram/ McClatchy-Tribune/Getty Images; p. 30 U.S. Navy/Getty Images News/Getty Images.

Printed in the United States of America

CPSIA compliance information: Batch # CW15GS: For further information contact Gareth Stevens, New York, New York at 1-800-542-2595.

CONTENTS

TAKING OFF

Military airplanes can do many different things. The US Air Force uses these planes all around the world. Some move people and supplies from place to place. Others are made to fight other aircraft. These are fighter planes!

Planes meant to attack things on the ground
are called bombers or attack aircraft.

Airplanes first took flight in 1909 when two brothers, Orville and Wilbur Wright, took off at Kitty Hawk, North Carolina. Airplanes were soon used by militaries and began to be used widely during World War I (1914–1918).

ORVILLE WRIGHT

WILBUR WRIGHT

Early airplanes used **propellers** to move forward and wings to create lift, which makes the plane rise off the ground.

SPAD TO THE BONE

One of the best fighter planes used in World War I was the SPAD. A French fighter plane, the SPAD VII was a biplane, which means it had two wings, and held one pilot. The Fokker Triplane—which had three wings—was used by German soldiers.

INTEL REPORT

SPAD was short for Société Pour L'Aviation et ses Dérivés, the French company that made them.

9

PLANES IN THE DOGFIGHT

World War II (1939–1945) brought new fighter planes and plans for air **combat**. Small, fast airplanes would shoot down enemy bombers to stop attacks. These planes would also fight one another. These battles were called dogfights.

INTEL REPORT

The British Royal Air Force often used
Supermarine Spitfire planes in
World War II dogfights.

Different countries had different planes during World War II. The United States used planes such as the P-51 Mustang or P-47 Thunderbolt. The Japanese had fighter planes called Zeroes, while the Messerschmitt Bf 109 was used in the German air force, called the Luftwaffe.

INTEL REPORT

Zero pilots would often crash their planes into ships and other targets on purpose. These were called kamikaze (kah-mih-KAH-zee) pilots.

P-51 MUSTANG

P-47 THUNDERBOLT

JAPANESE ZERO

MESSERSCHMITT BF 109

JET SETTING

The invention of the jet engine changed the way people took to the skies. Jet engines work by taking in a large amount of air and turning it into a high-speed jet of gas. This pushes the plane forward and makes it go very fast.

INTEL REPORT

Jet engines are used on most airplanes today
and let planes fly more than 7,000 miles
(11,265 km) per hour.

Jet fighters were made in the last days of World War II. The first major war that US Air Force jets were used in was the Korean War (1950–1953). The F-86 Sabre battled Russian-built MiG fighters, winning 10 battles for every 1 loss.

INTEL REPORT

The first jet fighter was the Me 262, which was used by the Germans in 1944.

As jets flew faster and faster, pilots also learned to avoid being spotted by the enemy. **Stealth** jets like the F-117 Nighthawk were built so they didn't show up on enemy **radar**. Many new jets started to use stealth **technology** in the 1980s and 1990s.

INTEL REPORT

The F-117 Nighthawk wasn't meant to be a fighter jet, but it was often called a "stealth fighter."

F-15

The F-15 was first used in 1972 and is still used today. Called the "Strike Eagle," it has two jet engines and room for two pilots. The F-15 can attack targets in the air as well as on the ground.

INTEL REPORT

Even with newer planes in the **fleet**, the US Air Force expects to use F-15s until at least 2019.

F-22 RAPTOR

The F-22 Raptor is part of the "fifth **generation**" of fighter jets. Two F119 engines, the most powerful in the world, help the F-22 fly around **Mach** 1.5 or more. The F-22 was first used by the US Air Force in 2012.

INTEL REPORT

The United States is the only country to
have a complete fleet of F-22 Raptors.

F-35

The newest jet in the US Air Force is the F-35. The F-35 seats a single pilot and can take off vertically, or straight up in the air, before moving forward! It also has advanced stealth technology and can take on many different roles for different branches of the military.

INTEL REPORT

The F-35 will be used by the air force,
Marine Corps, and navy in the
United States.

FUTURE JETS

The US military is already working on a plane to replace the F-22 and F-35. It will be a sixth-generation warplane. This plane will be able to fight others in the air as well as attack with missiles and other advanced weapons.

The sixth-generation jet is
supposed to be ready by 2030.

TODAY'S FIGHTERS

Today, many fighter planes are used for other things, such as dropping bombs and escorting other planes from place to place. There aren't many militaries that have fighter planes that can match the technology in the US Air Force's jets.

Many people think unmanned drones or unmanned jets can replace piloted fighters in the future.

INSIDE THE F-35 FIGHTER JET

COCKPIT

WING

WING

ENGINE

NAVY

F-35

CF-01

100

FOR MORE INFORMATION

Books

Hamilton, John. *F-22 Raptor*. Minneapolis, MN: ABDO Publishing, 2013.

Peppas, Lynn. *Fighter Jets: Defending the Skies*. New York, NY: Crabtree Publishing, 2012.

Von Finn, Denny. *F-35 Lightning IIs*. Minneapolis, MN: Bellwether Media, 2013.

Websites

Air Force History
airforce.com/learn-about/history/
Learn more about the history of fighter planes in the air force.

F-22 Raptor
f22-raptor.com
Get more information about one of the coolest fighter jets in the US Air Force.

F-35 Lightning II
f35.com
Read more about one of the newest planes in the US Air Force.

National Museum of the US Air Force
www.nationalmuseum.af.mil/research/aircraft/
Find more photos and stories about the fighter planes used in the US Air Force.

GLOSSARY

combat: armed fighting between opposing forces

fleet: a group of planes under one command

generation: a class of objects developed from an earlier type

Mach: a unit of measurement based on the speed of sound

propeller: a blade that turns quickly to move something forward

radar: a machine that uses radio waves to locate and identify objects

stealth: made to avoid being seen or spotted, or aiming not to be seen

technology: the way people do something using tools and the tools that they use

INDEX